To ....

From ....

Other books by Gregory E. Lang:

WHY A DAUGHTER NEEDS A DAD

WHY A SON NEEDS A MOM

WHY A SON NEEDS A DAD

WHY I LOVE GRANDMA

WHY I LOVE GRANDPA

WHY I CHOSE YOU

WHY I LOVE YOU

WHY MY HEART STILL SKIPS A BEAT

WHY I NEED YOU

WHY WE ARE A FAMILY

WHY WE ARE FRIENDS

GOOD LUCK, GRADUATE

BROTHERS AND SISTERS

SIMPLE ACTS

LOVE SIGNS

LIFE MAPS

THANK YOU, MOM

THANK YOU, DAD

BECAUSE YOU ARE MY DAUGHTER

BECAUSE YOU ARE MY SON

WHY A

Baby

NEEDS A

Mommy

100 REASONS

Gregory E. Lang

with photographs by Janet Lankford–Moran

CUMBERLAND HOUSE

Published by Cumberland House, an imprint of Sourcebooks, Inc.
P.O. Box 4410, Naperville, Illinois 60567–4410
(630) 961–3900
Fax: (630) 961–2168
www.sourcebooks.com

Printed and bound in China
OGP 10 9 8 7 6 5 4 3 2 1

TO MY MOM

——GREG

TO MY SWEET

LITTLE DOROTHY

——JANET

INTRODUCTION

P ERHAPS THE MOST joyous moment of my life was when I held my newborn daughter for the first time. In the world only a few minutes, a nurse held her out to me, wrapped snug in a keeping blanket. I eagerly but cautiously reached out and accepted her, taking great care to support her with both hands without holding her too tight, bringing her close to my chest to make sure I did not drop her, but not so close as to smoother her. I spoke to her in a near whisper, not wanting to startle her. "I love you," I said, before leaning down to kiss her forehead. Her sweet smell filled my lungs, her skin warmed my lips, and her cooing delighted my heart. In those few moments the lives of her mother and me changed forever.

In addition to that momentous day, we've had many other memorable moments with our little girl, like watching her take her first steps, feed herself for the first time (most of the spaghetti ended up on her shirt), the first evening she went to bed without diapers, and my favorite, hearing the first time she called me "Daddy." Nearly every day was fun and exciting, and yet nearly every day was challenging and at times stressful for either her mother or me.

She was our only child, and although we thought we had prepared ourselves well for her, we were fearful nonetheless, wondering if she was comfortable in our arms, was she wrapped too snug, was she hungry or sleepy. I had watched my mother take care of my younger siblings, and my aunts take care of my many younger cousins. My wife and I read books to educate ourselves about infants, we listened to family and friends as advice based on experience was given, and we took home and saved all the instructions the pediatrician had given us. Still, sometimes we didn't know what to do, so we learned by trial and error, trying to read facial expressions, interpret baby jabber, remember schedules, and anticipate what need might arise next. We were afraid we would do something wrong, we feared causing some long-lasting harm, and we struggled with our confidence on difficult days when we could not please our unhappy child.

There were times that we wondered out loud what she needed from us, when we disagreed about what to do, and when we tried anything we could think of to handle the challenge of the moment. There were times when we doubted our abilities as parents, when we wondered if our daughter would turn out all right, having been raised by inexperienced parents such as we were back then. There were times when I wanted desperately for her just to speak to us, to *tell* us what it was that she needed.

Those were the days that I wished she had come with a book, a parent's manual that described all possible infant behaviors and strange noises, reasons for tears, how to stop a runny nose, explanations for the different colors of poop and what to do for each one. Such a manual would have saved us a lot of frustration and doubt, a few temper tantrums, and perhaps made my daughter a bit more content with her parents. But alas, no such book existed.

We tried to be perfect parents. We took her to most of the places she wanted to go, bought all the stuffed animals that would fit in her room, gave her the snacks she demanded even though we didn't want her to have them, and read to her at night long after she could read for herself. But we did not do everything right. I'm sure we fell short more times than we would wish to count.

Fortunately, her mother and I learned from our successes as well as our mistakes, and from the insights we shared with each other. We learned that children are loving, resilient, and forgiving, but they are also delicate and impressionable. They will forgive us for most of our mistakes as long as our intentions were well-placed and we do better the next time, but they cannot thrive in our indifference, carelessness, or anger. We learned that children have many needs that require the purposeful service of devoted parents. While some of these needs are real only during early childhood, others endure for a lifetime and are staggering in their importance and effect if unattended. Some needs change, evolve, become less pressing, and others grow in importance as time goes by. Some needs must be met only once; others are never met but require constant feeding. Our children's own sense of worth is determined in large part by the worth they believe we have placed in them, which is demonstrated by how attentive we are to their needs instead of our own.

Today our young adult daughter cannot recall all the care that her parents gave her, yet she knows of it. That is why now and then when she visits either of us she still reaches for a hug before departing, or calls on the phone in near bursting exuberance to tell about something she has conquered that day. These are the moments when we are rewarded for what we did years ago; these are *more* of the moments, like those of her infancy and early childhood, we will remember for all of our remaining days. These are the moments when I can smile and believe that her mother and I have done a pretty good job as her parents.

We never did find that manual, so I decided to write one. I do not hold this book out as the exhaustive book of wisdom that all new parents need to read in order to raise perfect children. However, I believe that somewhere there are parents lying awake at night, as my child's mother and I once did, wondering what to do for their beloved baby. I hope that by sharing a bit about what I have learned, that giving a child a loving, supportive start in life, that taking care of a few basic, universal needs, those parents will find confidence in their abilities, comfort in their successes, and strength with each life lesson shared with their child. With this book I hope to give new parents, and especially moms, most often the primary caregiver, nurturer, and teacher, a glimpse of what they should know about and do for their young children. When you put this book down, I hope you feel encouraged and appreciated for all you have done and have yet to do taking care of your own precious baby.

WHY A

Baby

NEEDS A

Mommy

100 REASONS

I need
YOU

to remember that I am watching
everything you do.

I need
YOU

to know that the most comforting voice
in the world to me is yours.

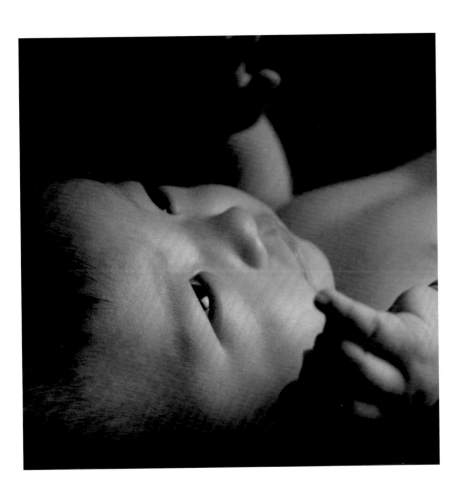

I need

YOU

....

to set an example for
me as I grow up.

....

I need
YOU

TO NEVER STOP LOVING ME.

·

to rub my back when I don't feel well.

·

TO KEEP MY STUFFED ANIMALS
NICE AND CLEAN.

·

to consider Grandma's advice. After all,
she has done this before.

I need YOU

to get me to eat the yucky stuff
that is good for me.

I need YOU

to prepare yourself for the changes
I am sure to go through.

I need
YOU

TO MAKE SURE SANTA CLAUS
KNOWS ABOUT ME.

.

*to remember to pack my blankie when
we leave the house.*

.

TO HELP ME LEARN HOW TO COUNT.

.

*to carry me on your shoulders
now and then.*

I need
YOU

to always remember that
I am only a child.

I need
YOU

to be patient with me
when I am frustrated.

I need
YOU

TO SING MY FAVORITE SONGS TO ME.

·

to play peek-a-boo with me.

·

TO MAKE SURE I AM ALWAYS
SNUG IN MY CAR SEAT.

·

*to make sure I put in my mouth
only what is supposed to go there.*

I need YOU

to make sure my toys
are just right for me.

I need YOU

....

to teach me all that you know.

....

I need YOU

....

to make sure my
bathwater isn't too hot.

....

I need YOU

to make time to play
with me every day.

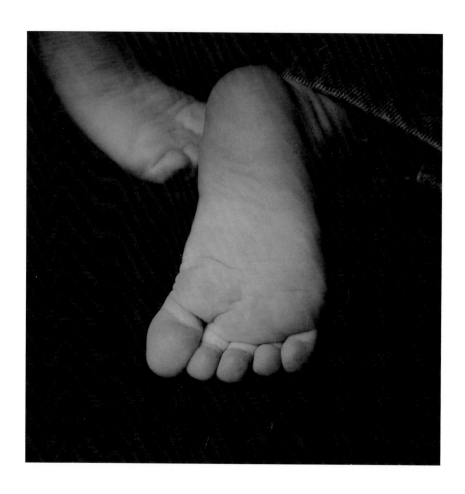

I need YOU

to keep out of my reach the things
I shouldn't play with.

I need
YOU

....

to understand that for a while things aren't going
to be as neat and orderly as they once were.

....

I need
YOU

TO CAREFULLY FOLLOW MY
DOCTOR'S INSTRUCTIONS.

.

to always be ready to catch me if I fall.

.

TO STIMULATE MY MIND. I WANT
TO BE AS SMART AS YOU ARE.

.

to pick me up when I reach for you.

$\mathcal{I}$ *need* YOU

to believe that you cannot
spoil me too much.

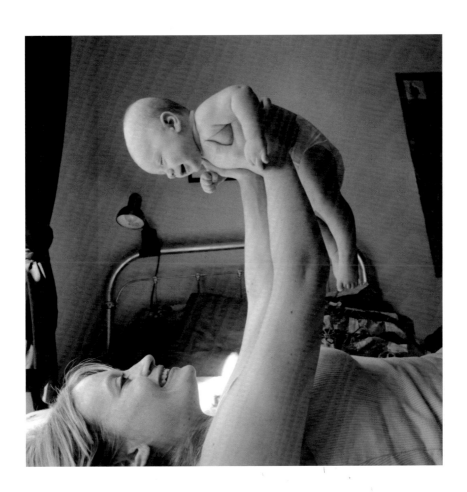

I need YOU

to introduce me to
our family traditions.

I need
YOU

to remember that sometimes the
simple pleasures are the most fun.

I need YOU

to make sure I have
lots of playmates.

I need YOU

NOT TO HOVER TOO MUCH—I NEED
TO TAKE CHANCES NOW AND THEN.

·

*to praise me when I do
something the right way.*

·

TO ROCK ME TO SLEEP ONCE IN A WHILE.

·

to speak to me in a soft, slow voice.

I need
YOU

to encourage me when
I try to do new things.

I need YOU

to remember that I want to
be included in everything.

$\mathcal{I}$ need
YOU

....

to read to me often.

....

I need
YOU

TO LET ME GROW UP—I CAN'T
BE A BABY FOREVER.

·

to make sure I learn good manners.

·

TO HELP ME UNDERSTAND WHY
I CAN'T ALWAYS HAVE MY WAY.

·

to always accept my affection.

I need YOU

to understand that I cannot tell time.
To me, everything is "now."

I need
YOU

....

to protect me from the weather.

....

I need
YOU

TO KEEP A WATCHFUL EYE ON ME.

·

to comfort me when I am afraid.

·

TO KISS ME OFTEN.

·

to understand that I didn't intend
to wake you, I just missed you.

I need YOU

....

to keep me clean and smelling fresh.

....

I need YOU

to carry me when I am tired.

I need YOU

....

to take me outside and explore
the world with me.

....

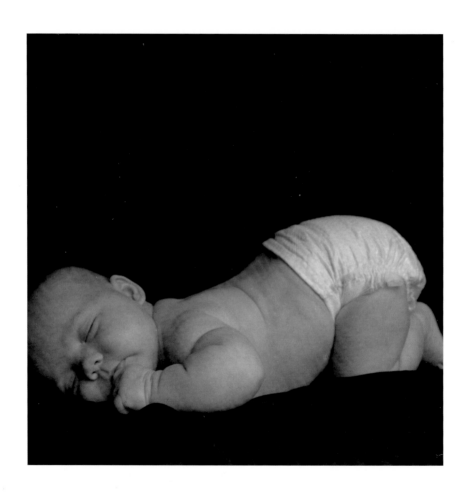

I need
YOU

....

to make sure I don't skip my naps.

....

I need
YOU

to introduce me to
everyone in our family.

I need YOU

to learn my language until
I can speak yours.

I need
YOU

to remember that my
feelings can be easily hurt.

I need
YOU

....

to reassure me that you are glad I am here.

....

I need
YOU

TO PREPARE YOURSELF FOR HOW YOUR
LIFE WILL CHANGE WITH ME IN IT.

·

to understand that sometimes
all I know to do is cry.

·

TO REMEMBER THAT THERE ARE
SOME THINGS THAT I AM JUST
TOO YOUNG TO SEE.

·

to understand that while you might be
tired of it, I'm thrilled to do it again.
And again. And again.

I need

YOU

....

to remember where I left
my favorite toy.

....

I need YOU

....

to snuggle with me often.

....

I need YOU

to tickle me, but not too much.

I need
YOU

TO LET ME HOLD YOUR HAND
WHENEVER I WANT TO.

.

to take a nap with me once in a while.

.

TO RESIST TAKING EMBARRASSING
PHOTOGRAPHS OF ME.

.

to resist dressing me in weird outfits.

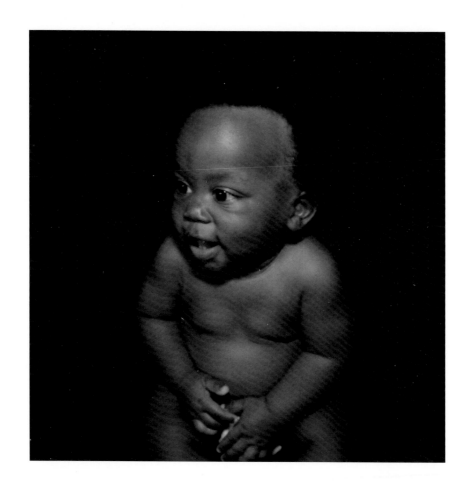

I need YOU

to remember that I am
always counting on you.

I need YOU

to come to me when I call for you.

I *need* YOU

to forgive me for the stress I am sure
to cause you from time to time.

I need
YOU

TO BELIEVE THAT ONE DAY I WILL BE
ABLE TO THANK YOU FOR ALL THAT
YOU HAVE DONE FOR ME.

·

not to worry about your mistakes—
I won't remember them.

·

NOT TO WORRY ABOUT BEING
PERFECT—I WON'T BE EITHER.

·

to remember that what I want to
hear most is "I love you."

I need
YOU

....

to remember that I like fun surprises.

....

I need YOU

TO TAKE GOOD CARE OF YOURSELF SO
THAT YOU'LL HAVE ENOUGH ENERGY
TO KEEP UP WITH ME.

·

*to remember that I can't help having
little accidents now and then.*

·

TO UNDERSTAND THAT IT WOULD
FRIGHTEN ME IF YOU WERE TO
GET ANGRY WITH ME.

·

to make sure to save some time for yourself.

I need
YOU

to believe that I love you
as much as you love me.

I need
YOU

to understand that it's okay to leave me
as long as you always come back for me.

I need
YOU

to teach me how to play patty-cake.

I need
YOU

TO MAKE SURE OUR HOME
IS SAFE FOR ME.

·

to keep my baby book up-to-date.

·

TO TUCK ME IN WITH A KISS AT NIGHT.

·

*to teach me how to do the things I will
one day need to do for myself.*

I need YOU

to remember how much I love
to discover new things.

I need
YOU

TO UNDERSTAND THAT JUST BECAUSE
IT DOESN'T SCARE YOU DOESN'T MEAN
IT WON'T SCARE ME.

·

*to give me all the affection you
want to—it'll never be too much.*

·

TO UNDERSTAND THAT SOME THINGS HAVE
CHANGED SINCE YOU WERE MY AGE.

·

*to love me the most when I don't
seem to love you at all.*

I need YOU

to make sure I have plenty
of room to move around.

I need YOU

because without you I don't
know what I'd do.

· ACKNOWLEDGMENTS ·

I ENJOY THE SUPPORT of many people, which is the only reason I am able to accomplish much of anything worthwhile. To them a heartfelt thanks is given—to Dominique Raccah and the awesome staff at Sourcebooks, I am blessed by your endless support; to my very talented friend Janet Moran, who took the photographs of the precious faces adorning this book; to Jill, my wife, for her unlimited love, support, and encouragement; and to our beautiful daughters Meagan and Linley, who remind me daily of the joys of parenting two slobbering babes in arms through to the beautiful young women they've become. Girls—you are loved more than you can fathom.

TO CONTACT THE AUTHOR

Write in care of the publisher:
Gregory E. Lang c/o Sourcebooks, Inc.
P.O. Box 4410
Naperville, IL 60567-4410

Email the author or visit his website:
gregoryelang@gmail.com
www.gregoryelang.com

Email the photographer or visit her website:
janetlmoran@gmail.com
www.oijoyphoto.com